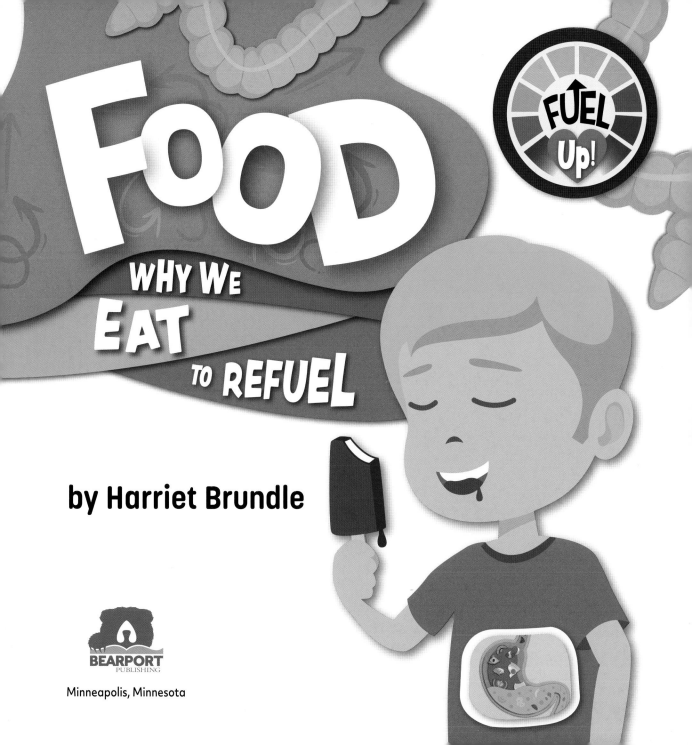

FOOD

WHY WE EAT TO REFUEL

FUEL Up!

by Harriet Brundle

BEARPORT
PUBLISHING

Minneapolis, Minnesota

Library of Congress Cataloging-in-Publication Data

Names: Brundle, Harriet, author.
Title: Food : why we eat to refuel / by Harriet Brundle.
Description: Fusion. | Minneapolis, MN : Bearport Publishing Company, [2021] | Series: Fuel up! | Includes bibliographical references and index.
Identifiers: LCCN 2020009778 (print) | LCCN 2020009779 (ebook) | ISBN 9781647473433 (library binding) | ISBN 9781647473488 (paperback) | ISBN 9781647473532 (ebook)
Subjects: LCSH: Nutrition–Juvenile literature. | Food–Juvenile literature.
Classification: LCC RA784 .B747 2021 (print) | LCC RA784 (ebook) | DDC 613.2–dc23
LC record available at https://lccn.loc.gov/2020009778
LC ebook record available at https://lccn.loc.gov/2020009779

CONTENTS

ALL ABOUT FOOD

Food is a very important type of **fuel**. Our bodies need food every day. Each time you eat, you are giving your body the fuel it needs to work.

Different types of food give our bodies the **nutrients** we need. It's important to eat the right food each day to stay healthy.

WHERE DOES MY FOOD GO?

You chew food with your teeth. Then, you swallow it.

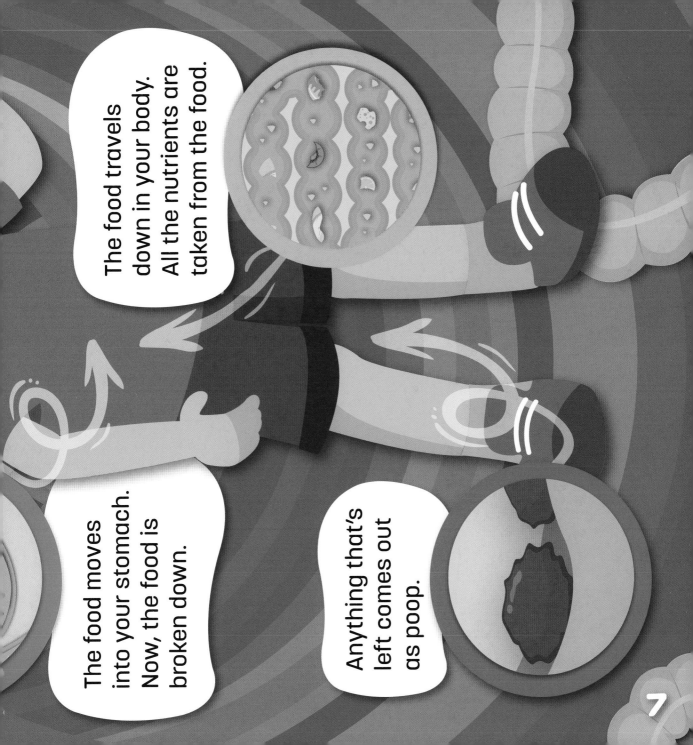

The food travels down in your body. All the nutrients are taken from the food.

The food moves into your stomach. Now, the food is broken down.

Anything that's left comes out as poop.

7

FOOD GROUPS

The food we eat is split into different groups. Each group gives our bodies different nutrients.

Carbs are a group with foods such as bread, pasta, rice, potatoes, and oats. Our bodies use carbs for energy.

Protein is found in foods such as meat, fish, and nuts. Foods in the protein group help our bodies grow and fix themselves.

Dairy group foods include milks, yogurts, and cheeses. These foods have a lot of **calcium**, which helps us have strong bones and teeth.

Fruits and vegetables give our bodies lots of different nutrients. These groups keep our bodies healthy.

Fats and sugars are groups found in foods such as chips, cookies, sodas, and cakes. It's best not to have too much of this type of food.

WHY DO I NEED FOOD?

When you haven't eaten anything for a few hours, you start to feel hungry. Your tummy might rumble, and you might feel dizzy or find it hard to pay attention.

If you stopped eating food, you would start to feel sick. It's important to eat enough to keep your body well fueled.

IF YOU FEEL HUNGRY, SPEAK TO AN ADULT.

13

WHAT IS A BALANCED DIET?

BREAD

A **balanced** diet should have between three and five servings of carbs each day.

PASTA

POTATOES

CHICKEN

We should have around two servings of protein each day.

CHICKPEAS

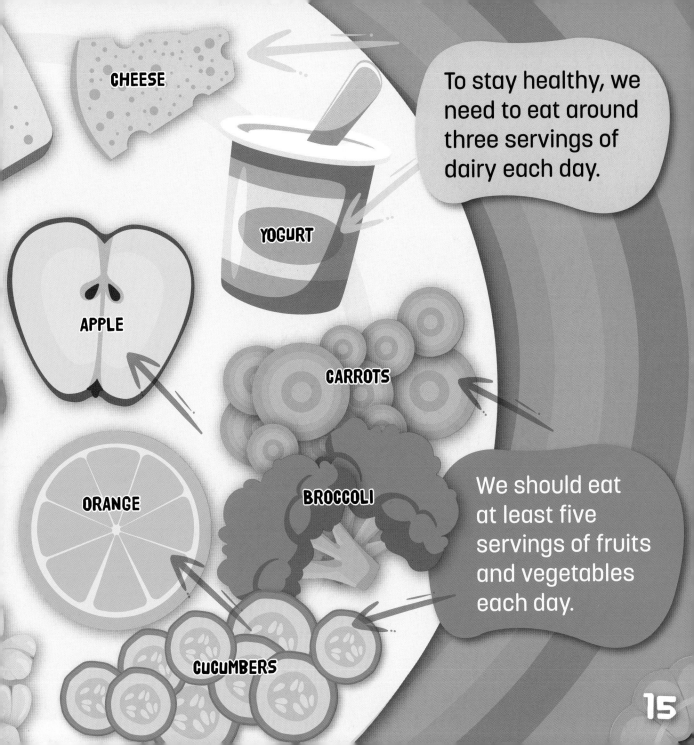

CHEESE

YOGURT

APPLE

CARROTS

ORANGE

BROCCOLI

CUCUMBERS

To stay healthy, we need to eat around three servings of dairy each day.

We should eat at least five servings of fruits and vegetables each day.

TOO MUCH FAT AND SUGAR

Eating too much food with lots of fat and sugar can give you a stomachache or make you gain weight. Lots of sugar can also be bad for your teeth.

If you feel hungry, try having a healthy snack to refuel your body.

CARROT STICKS ARE A TASTY, HEALTHY SNACK!

EXERCISE

The food we eat gives us the fuel we need to be able to play, run, and jump. Exercise is also an important part of staying healthy.

DRINKING

Drinking plenty of water is an important part of fueling your body. Have a drink every time you eat and anytime you feel thirsty in between.

IF IT'S A WARM DAY OR IF YOU'VE DONE LOTS OF EXERCISE, YOU SHOULD DRINK MORE WATER.

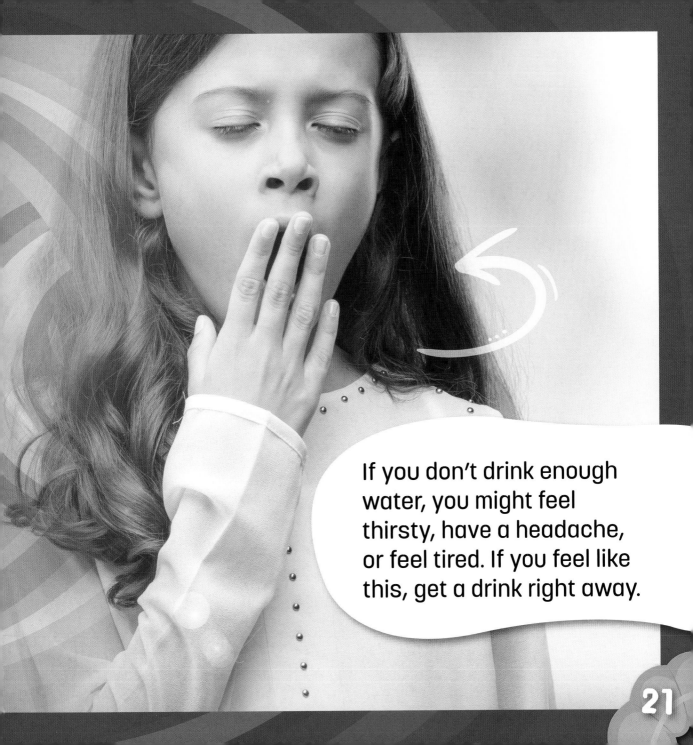

If you don't drink enough water, you might feel thirsty, have a headache, or feel tired. If you feel like this, get a drink right away.

21

Fuel Up with Food!

This plate shows how many servings of each food group we need to eat each day to stay healthy.

Make a list of what you have eaten so far today. Which groups were each of the foods a part of? Are there any food groups you haven't had enough servings of today?

FRUIT

DAIRY

CARBS

FATS

GLOSSARY

balanced the right amount of things

calcium something found in some types of food as well as in your bones and teeth

carbs short for carbohydrates, these nutrients give the body energy

fuel something that can be used to make energy or power something

muscles the parts of the body that are used to cause movement

nutrients natural substances that plants and animals need to grow and stay healthy

organs parts of a living thing that have specific, important jobs to do

protein a nutrient used to help the body grow and to fix things in the body that are broken

INDEX